The Moody GUIDE TO THE BIBLE

by Tim Dowley

Illustrations by Richard Scott

Moody Press
Chicago

The Bible
– many books in one

We are used to thinking of the Bible as a single large book, but as soon as we open a Bible it becomes clear that it is in fact a collection of books – sixty-six in all. Some are long, some very short; some were written in the time of the Roman Empire, some centuries earlier. The books vary too in their contents; some consist of history, others of poetry, others of wise sayings, and some are personal letters.

The Bible is, of course, divided into two sections, the Old Testament and the New Testament (see p.24 for New Testament).

Old Testament

The Old Testament – the first thirty-nine books of the Bible – is made up of the scriptures of the Jews. It was originally written in Hebrew or Aramaic, but we no longer have any of the original copies. In fact, until 1947 we did not know of any copies of the Old Testament that dated from before the ninth century AD. However, in that year the famous Dead Sea Scrolls were discovered; they were found to consist of copies of all the Old

Right: The caves where the Dead Sea Scrolls were discovered.

Below: Two copper scrolls from Qumran.

Testament books except Esther, and date from about the time of Christ.

The Dead Sea Scrolls, which belonged to the library of a Jewish religious community living at Qumran, near the Dead Sea, were very important in showing that there had been very few changes in the words of the Old Testament over hundreds of years.

We are not certain how the Old Testament came together as a single collection of books, but we know that the Jews grouped them into three sections:
1. The Law: the first five books of the Old Testament
2. The Prophets: the writings of the prophets such as Ezekiel and Isaiah, and also books of history such as 1 and 2 Kings
3. The Writings: books such as Proverbs and Job, with their wise sayings, and also later books of history, such as Chronicles and Ezra.

Christians usually divide up the Old Testament into four groups of books:
1. The Law: Genesis – Deuteronomy
2. History: Joshua – Esther
3. Wisdom: Job – Song of Songs
4. Prophets: Isaiah – Malachi

Genesis Exodus Leviticus Numbers Deuteronomy Joshua Judges Ruth 1 Samuel 2 Samuel 1 Kings 2 Kings 1 Chronicles 2 Chronicles Ezra Nehemiah Esther

The Law   **History**

Translating the Bible

In the third century BC, seventy Jewish scholars set about translating the Old Testament into Greek. This was the first translation of any part of the Bible. Later, parts of the New Testament were translated into the Coptic and Syriac languages, and Jerome produced a version of the Bible in Latin.

In England, a monk called Bede translated parts of the Bible into Anglo-Saxon, the language of the people. English translations followed, by John Wycliffe, and by William Tyndale, around the time of the Reformation.

During the last two centuries there have been many more English translations, and the Bible has also been translated into most of the major languages of the world.

The British and Foreign Bible Society was founded in 1804 and soon started to translate the Bible into new languages. It was followed by national Bible Societies in the Netherlands, Scotland and the United States, and many other countries.

Since World War II, a new society called the Wycliffe Bible Translators has undertaken the huge task of translating the Bible into the tribal languages of many remote peoples of the world.

Above: A monk copies a biblical manuscript, adding elaborate decorations.

Right: William Carey was a pioneering English Baptist missionary to India. He was an evangelist and educationist, and supervised six complete and twenty-four partial translations of the Bible.

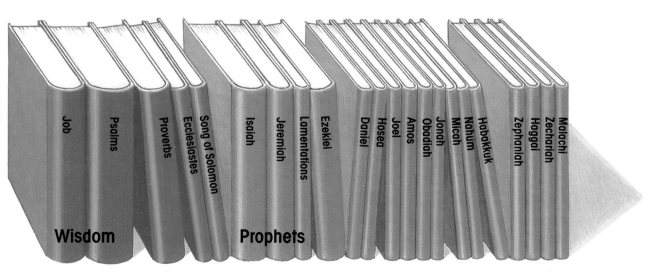

Job · Psalms · Proverbs · Ecclesiastes · Song of Solomon · Isaiah · Jeremiah · Lamentations · Ezekiel · Daniel · Hosea · Joel · Amos · Obadiah · Jonah · Micah · Nahum · Habakkuk · Zephaniah · Haggai · Zechariah · Malachi

Wisdom   **Prophets**

The Story of God's People

Abraham becomes
a tent-dweller

Abram leaves Ur

Joseph taken
to Egypt

The Israeli[tes]
occupy the
Promised Land

Moses receives
the Ten Commandments

Jacob's family
settle in Egypt

The Exodus

2000 BC
1900
1800
1700
1600
1500
1400
1300
1200
1100

The first chapters of the book of Genesis are set in Mesopotamia, the traditional site of the Garden of Eden and the Tower of Babel, which was probably built like a ziggurat, or temple tower. From Mesopotamia, Abraham set out on his great journey to the Promised Land.

Abraham, and later his grandson Jacob, were both driven into Egypt by famine. The Israelites, descendants of Jacob (or Israel), settled there, increased in number, and were enslaved by the Egyptians. Their escape from Egypt, led by Moses, is recounted in the book of Exodus.

The next forty years were spent in the harsh Sinai Desert; here the Israelites were given the Ten Commandments and their complex system of laws, set down in Exodus, Leviticus, Numbers and Deuteronomy.

The Promised Land

After they had conquered the land of Canaan, the Israelites divided up the territory among the tribes and settled it. The story of their struggle with surrounding tribes is told in Judges.

As the nation developed, there was a succession of kings, starting with Saul. The history of the kingdom and its division is told in Samuel, Kings and Chronicles. During King Solomon's reign, the first Temple was built in Jerusalem.

Exile

With the rise of Assyria, Israel was threatened with invasion and exile. A number of prophets, notably Isaiah, warned of this peril, seeing it as a mark of God's judgment on the nation's sin. Eventually the people of the northern kingdom (Israel) were taken into exile.

The southern kingdom (Judah) and the city of Jerusalem itself fell to Babylonia. Jeremiah

Between the Testaments

There was a gap of 400 years from the time when the last book of the Old Testament was written till the time when Jesus was born. It was a time when no prophets arose to speak God's message to his people.

During this time, the Jews were constantly under pressure from two empires – from the Seleucids who ruled Syria, and from the Ptolemies who ruled Egypt in the south.

A low point came under the rule of Antiochus Epiphanes, who suspended the Temple sacrifices, ordered the Scriptures to be destroyed and forbade the Jews to observe the Sabbath.

The Jews organized a strong resistance, led first by the high priest, Mattathias, and later by his three sons Judas 'the hammer' (Maccabaeus), Jonathan and Simon.

Israel taken captive to Assyria

Israel has first king

King Jeroboam

King Saul

ISRAEL

Samaria is destroyed

The kingdom divides

Solomon builds First Temple

King Rehoboam

JUDAH

Jerusalem and the Temple destroyed

Second Temple built

The Temple desecrated by Antiochus Epiphanes

Herod's Temple built

Some return from exile

Jeremiah warns Judah

Walls of Jerusalem repaired

Judah taken captive by Babylon

Ezra and Nehemiah return to Jerusalem

Birth of Jesus

Ezekiel prophesies

Judah in exile

Judas 'the hammer' Maccabaeus fights for freedom

900 800 700 600 500 400 300 200 100 0

prophesied amidst this disaster, while the prophet Ezekiel, in exile, recalled his people to their God.

The Jews later returned by stages to their own land and rebuilt Jerusalem and the Temple (Ezra, Nehemiah).

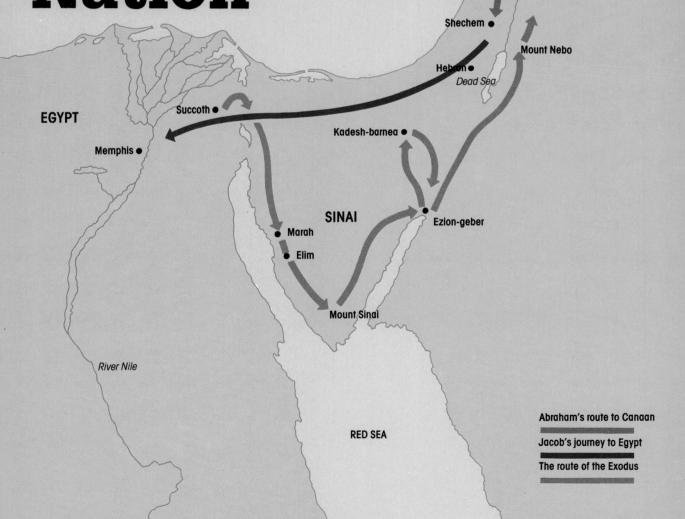

8

MEDITERRANEAN SEA

Fathers of the Nation

CANAAN

Shechem ●

Mount Nebo

Hebron ●
Dead Sea

EGYPT

Succoth ●

Kadesh-barnea ●

Memphis ●

SINAI

Ezion-geber

Marah ●

Elim ●

Mount Sinai

River Nile

RED SEA

Abraham's route to Canaan

Jacob's journey to Egypt

The route of the Exodus

● Haran

A shepherd tends his flock in an oasis near Ur, Abraham's birthplace.

River Euphrates

BABYLONIA

● Babylon

River Tigris

ARABIAN DESERT

Ur

Abraham

Abraham was brought up in Ur in Babylonia, on the river Euphrates. Called by God, he left Ur with his father, Terah, and travelled north to Haran. God promised to give the land of Canaan to Abraham and his descendants, so he journeyed on to the 'Promised Land' (Genesis 11–12).

Abraham settled in Canaan at Mamre, near Hebron, briefly visiting Egypt when famine came. Abraham's wife Sarah gave birth to a son, Isaac, in old age, so fulfilling God's promise to make Abraham the father of a great nation (Genesis 18, 21).

Jacob

Isaac married Rebekah and had two sons, Esau and Jacob. Jacob, the younger son, won the inheritance by deceiving Isaac.

He left Canaan and went back to Haran, returning years later with two wives and twelve sons (Genesis 25, 27, 29).

Joseph

Jacob's favourite son, Joseph, was sold as a slave by his jealous brothers. Taken to Egypt, he was imprisoned on a faked charge, but then rose to become a chief minister of the Pharaoh. When famine came to Canaan, Jacob and the rest of his family migrated to Egypt, where they prospered (Genesis 37, 42–46).

Moses

The Israelites stayed in Egypt for some four hundred years. Jacob's family grew into a nation, and the Egyptians no longer welcomed them, but forced them to work as slaves. God sent Moses as a leader to set his people free.

Moses eventually led the Israelites out of Egypt, but only after the country had been struck with a series of terrible disasters. The Israelites spent forty years in the desert, where Moses died, before entering the Promised Land (Exodus).

The Tent of Meeting

After the Exodus, while they were on their way from Egypt to Canaan, the Israelites worshipped God in a great tent (sometimes called the Tabernacle). When they set up camp in a new site, the Levites, who assisted the priests, erected the Tent of Meeting in the middle, with their own tents around it, and the tents of the tribes of Israel encircling them. In this way they showed that the worship of God was central to their nation's life.

The Tent of Meeting was constructed upon a framework of acacia wood, and measured about 14 metres (45 feet) long, 4 metres (13 feet) wide and 5 metres (15 feet) high. It was covered with four separate layers of material: decorated linen curtains, goats'-hair curtains, rams'-skin coverings, and a final water-proof animal-skin covering.

Inside the Tent
Inside the Tent were two rooms, the smaller one further from the entrance. This was the Holiest Place, which was entered only by the high priest only once a year.

Inside the Holiest Place stood the Ark of the Covenant, a rectangular wooden box, overlaid with gold, and containing the two stone tablets of the Ten Commandments, a pot of manna and Aaron's rod.

In front of the Holiest Place stood the altar of incense, where incense was burned every morning and evening, and a seven-branched lampstand. Each Sabbath, or day of rest, twelve loaves were placed on the table of showbread, one for each tribe, as an offering to God.

Outside the Tent
The Tent itself was surrounded by a curtained-off courtyard roughly 50 metres (150 feet) long and 25 metres (75 feet) wide, where the priests prepared the sacrifices. In front of the Tent stood a huge bronze basin where the priests ritually washed themselves, and the altar where sacrifices of goats, bulls, lambs and other animals were burned.

The Tent and all its furniture were made so that they could easily be packed up and carried to another site. The Tent of Meeting and its rituals are described in detail in Exodus 35–40 and Leviticus.

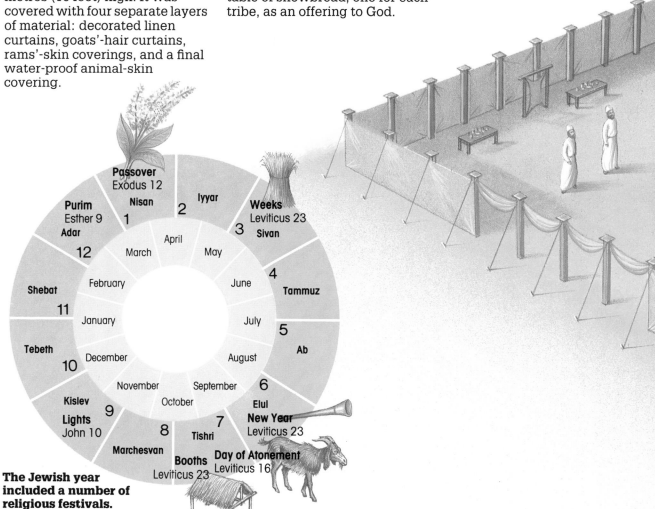

The Jewish year included a number of religious festivals.

The Religious Festivals

Passover – when Jewish families remembered together God's sparing the lives of their firstborn, in Egypt (Exodus 12). The Passover meal, with its unleavened bread, reminded them of the hurried departure from Egypt at the Exodus (Leviticus 23:5–14).

First-fruits – when the first sheaf of the barley harvest was presented to God.

Weeks (or Pentecost) – a time of thanksgiving at the end of the harvest (Leviticus 23:15–22).

New Year (or Trumpets) – the first day of the seventh month; a day of rest (Leviticus 23:23–25).

Day of Atonement – the day of national confession, when the high priest entered the Holiest Place and sprinkled the blood from the sacrifice (Leviticus 23:26–32).

Booths (or Tabernacles) – a joyful festival marking the end of the fruit harvest. Families would build huts from tree branches and live in them for the days of the feast (Leviticus 23:33–43).

Later, two additional festivals were included in the Jewish calendar:

Lights (or Dedication – today known as Hanukkah) – marking the cleansing of the Second Temple after it had been polluted. Each evening lights were placed in homes and synagogues.

Purim – a noisy festival remembering the time when Queen Esther saved her people from massacre (Esther).

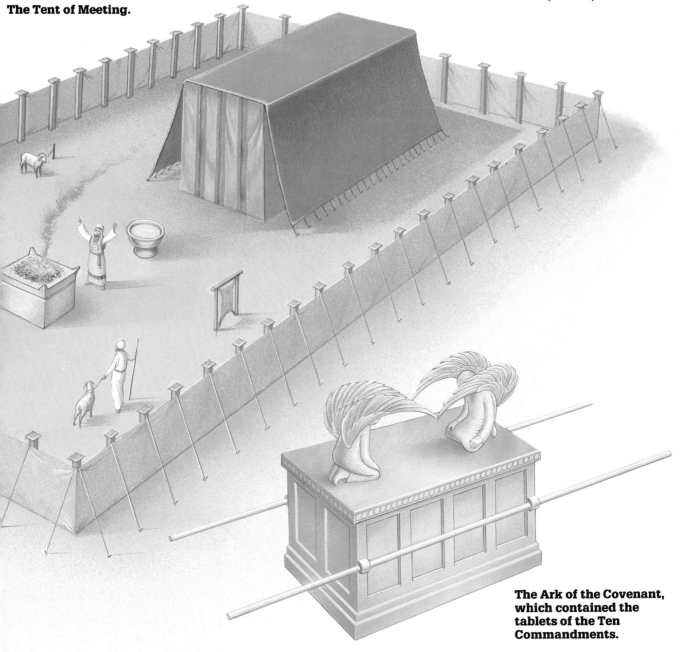

The Tent of Meeting.

The Ark of the Covenant, which contained the tablets of the Ten Commandments.

Israel
in Old Testament Times

One main road led across the country: it ran from Damascus through Galilee and across the Valley of Jezreel towards Mount Carmel, then down the flat coastal strip to Egypt. Because this road ran across her territories, the kingdom of Israel always had a stream of foreigners travelling through who greatly influenced her affairs.

The coast of Palestine has no good natural harbours, and in Old Testament times the hostile Philistines often occupied the southern part of the coast.

Apart from the river Jordan, Palestine has few rivers. The main rains fall in autumn and spring, but in the south amount to very little. Water is precious.

MEDITERRANEAN SEA

Dan

Hazor

Sea of Galilee

Tyre

PHOENICIA

Shunem

Jezreel

Beth Shan

Megiddo

Samaria

Shechem

ISRAEL

Mount Carmel

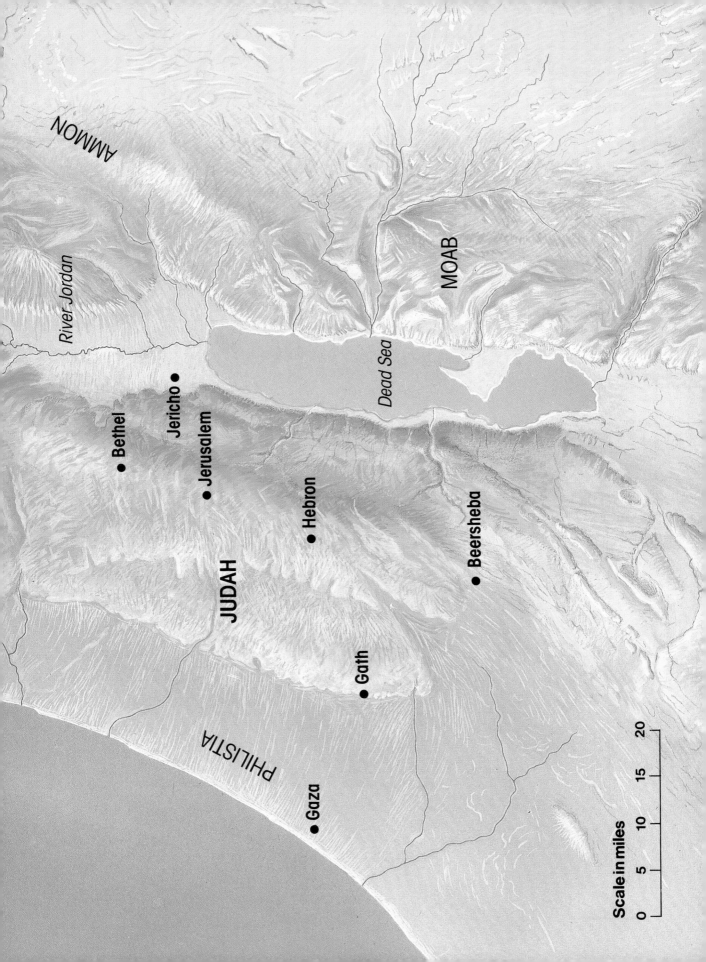

AMMON

River Jordan

MOAB

Dead Sea

Bethel

Jericho

Jerusalem

Hebron

Beersheba

JUDAH

Gath

PHILISTIA

Gaza

Scale in miles

0   5   10   15   20

Months of Jewish year

1 Nisan	2 Iyyar	3 Sivan	4 Tammuz	5 Ab	6 Elul

Spring
Late rain

Dry season begins

Summer figs

Barley harvest
Flax harvest

Early figs ripen

Grape harvest

Olive harvest

Dates

The Farmer's Year

In Bible times, almost everybody was involved in farming. Most households had their small plot of land, kept a few animals and grew crops.

Agriculture
The Israelites grew mainly wheat and barley. After the autumn rains had softened the ground, the farmer would use a simple wooden plough pulled by oxen to turn over the soil. He then sowed the grain by hand and ploughed the seed into the soil. If the winter rains came, the crop would be ready for harvesting in April or May.

The farmer cut his crops with a hand-held sickle and tied the stalks into sheaves, which were left in the fields to dry. Often stray stalks were left for the poor to gather up for food.

If the winter rains did not come, no grain would appear, and there would be no bread. Swarms of locusts or foreign armies could also destroy a farmer's crops.

Threshing
After the sheaves had been tied, they were taken to an open-air threshing floor where the crop was spread and oxen trod the grains out of the ears. Sometimes the oxen dragged over the grain a heavy wooden board studded with stone or iron spikes.

Next the farmer winnowed the crop by throwing it in the air with a pitchfork; the wind would blow away the chaff, but the heavier grain would fall near his feet.

Finally, the farmer winnowed his grain again, with a sieve, before putting it into a sack or an earthenware jar for storage.

Fruit
For the Israelites, the most important fruit crops were grapes, olives and figs. Olive trees and grape-vines grew on the sunny hillsides. Grapes were used to make wine, and olives to

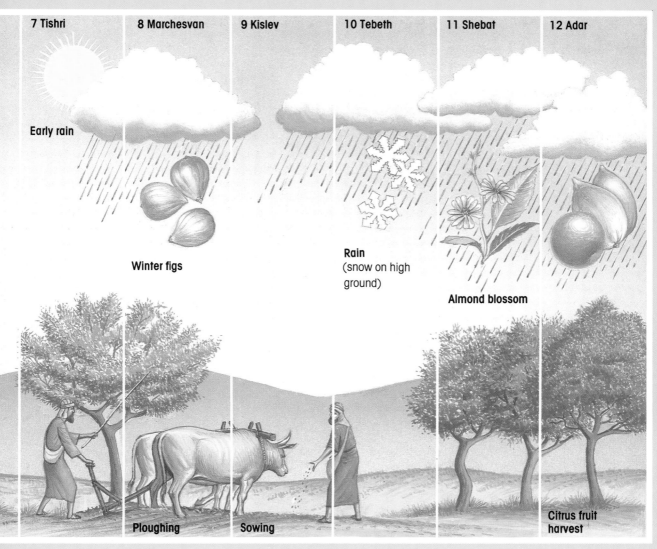

7 Tishri — Early rain

8 Marchesvan — Winter figs

9 Kislev

10 Tebeth — Rain (snow on high ground)

11 Shebat — Almond blossom

12 Adar

Ploughing

Sowing

Citrus fruit harvest

A woman cuts grain with a sickle in the traditional way.

make oil. Farmers also grew other fruit such as melons, dates, pomegranates and nuts.

Vegetables
Farmers in Israel also grew vegetables such as onions, cucumbers, lentils, beans, garlic and herbs. These would be cultivated close to their houses, or sometimes between the rows of vines.

Animals
Farmers kept animals such as sheep, goats, oxen and asses; the sheep were often herded together with the goats. Sheep were kept to give wool for making clothes, and were sometimes killed for their meat. Sheep's milk was drunk by the poorest people.

Costume

Most people living in Bible times wore quite simple clothing. The basic male garment was the loincloth, which men of all ranks wore. Over this, men usually wore an inner and an outer garment. The inner garment was normally of linen or wool, and long-sleeved; it would be fastened by a belt, and reach to the knees or ankles.

The outer garment, worn over this, was usually a square-shaped cloak made of animal skin or wool. The wearer would drape this cloak over one or both shoulders, and a man was reckoned to be naked without it. At night he would take it off and use it as a bed covering.

Wealthy men would often wear outer garments of beautifully-embroidered fine linen.

Priests' clothing

The priest wore a linen garment, tied with a belt of twisted blue, purple and scarlet linen, and a white linen head-covering.

The high priest had a much more elaborate garment worked in gold, purple and scarlet, and a breastplate inlaid with twelve precious stones, one for each of the twelve tribes.

The king of Israel also sometimes wore a tunic like that of a priest, together with a distinctive head-dress.

Women's clothing

Like the men, women wore simple under-garments, though these were higher at the neck and often reached down to the ankles. Women's clothes were generally white, though some wore black or blue. Rich women, like their husbands, wore fine linen, dyed bright red or purple, and they decorated their clothes with jewels, silver, gold and intricate embroidery. Women probably also wore simple head-coverings rather like modern prayer-shawls, and veils held down by strings of coins.

In Old Testament times, Jewish men tended to grow beards and wear their hair long; later, influenced by the Greeks and Romans, they wore their hair shorter.

A peasant.

A peasant woman with her child.

A rich man.

Making the cloth

The main materials used for making clothes were sheep's wool, goats' hair, animal skins and linen.

To make linen, flax had to be cut and dried, soaked and then dried again. Then the fibres were separated, and the flax could be spun and woven into cloth.

Making woollen cloth was another complicated process. First a fuller washed or cleaned the wool, using special chemicals. Then it was usually dyed with natural dyes, using potash and lime to fix the dyes and stop them running. Now the wool was ready to be spun and woven. Spinning was usually done simply by women using hand spindles, and then the weaving was carried out on a vertical or horizontal loom, in the same way as for linen and goats' hair.

Washing the clothes

Clothes were cleaned by putting them in a fast-running stream, so that the dirt was washed out of the cloth, or by wetting the clothes and then pounding them hard on flat stones to beat out the dirt. The women would use soap made of olive oil or vegetables.

Make-up and jewels

Men and women would adorn themselves with rings and pendants, often set with precious stones. Women wore make-up made of natural minerals such as kohl and galena. They would also paint their fingernails and toenails with oil-based colours. Make-up was applied either with the fingers, or with a special tool called a spatula.

At her wedding, a bride wore an elaborate head-dress.

A shepherd.

A soldier.

A high priest.

The Temple

Once the Israelites had conquered Canaan, they stopped carrying the Tent of Meeting about with them. King David finally brought the Ark of the Covenant to Jerusalem and planned to build a temple there, even buying the site for it. But it was his son Solomon who actually supervised the building of the first Temple.

Much the same in plan as the Tent of Meeting, the Temple was considerably larger. It measured about 9 metres (30 feet) wide, 27 metres (87 feet) long, and 13.5 metres (43 feet) high. A full description of it appears in 1 Kings 5–7.

Built of stone, it was totally covered inside with elaborately-decorated cedar panels, carved with flowers, palms and cherubim. The timber used in its construction was specially imported from Lebanon in the north.

Inside the Temple

Like the Tent of Meeting, the Temple housed the altar of incense, the table of showbread, lampstands, and, in the Holiest Place, the Ark of the Covenant.

The Temple was only very dimly lighted inside, by means of windows high up in the walls and special lampstands; the Holiest Place was completely dark, having neither windows nor lamps.

The rituals carried out in the Temple were similar to those laid down for the Tent of Meeting. The priests burned incense inside the Temple, and outside in the courtyard made the sacrifices that were demanded by the Law.

The Temple was not a cathedral-sized building, since it was designed as a house for God, not a meeting place for his people, and only the priests were allowed entry.

This model of Herod's Temple has been constructed in the grounds of a Jerusalem hotel.

Solomon held a great service of dedication when the Temple was completed. The building then became a focus for Jewish worship. But when the ten tribes broke away to form the northern kingdom, they set up temples of their own elsewhere.

Solomon's Temple was finally destroyed by King Nebuchadnez-zar of Babylon when he captured the city of Jerusalem in 586/587 BC, taking the people into captivity.

Cyrus the Great, Emperor of Persia, eventually let the Jews return to Jerusalem, and, encouraged by the prophets Haggai and Zechariah, the people set about rebuilding the Temple, probably on a less grand scale than Solomon's. Cyrus also returned to the Jews the gold and silver objects taken from the Temple, so that it could once again be finely furnished.

This rebuilt Temple was itself destroyed, by the Roman general Pompey in 63 BC.

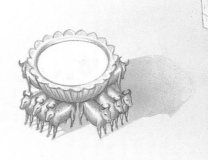

Herod's Temple

In 19 BC, Herod the Great started to build a magnificent new Temple in Jerusalem. It was on the same plan as Solomon's Temple, but was easily the grandest of the three. Twice the height of Solomon's Temple, it was covered with gold, and shimmered in the sun.

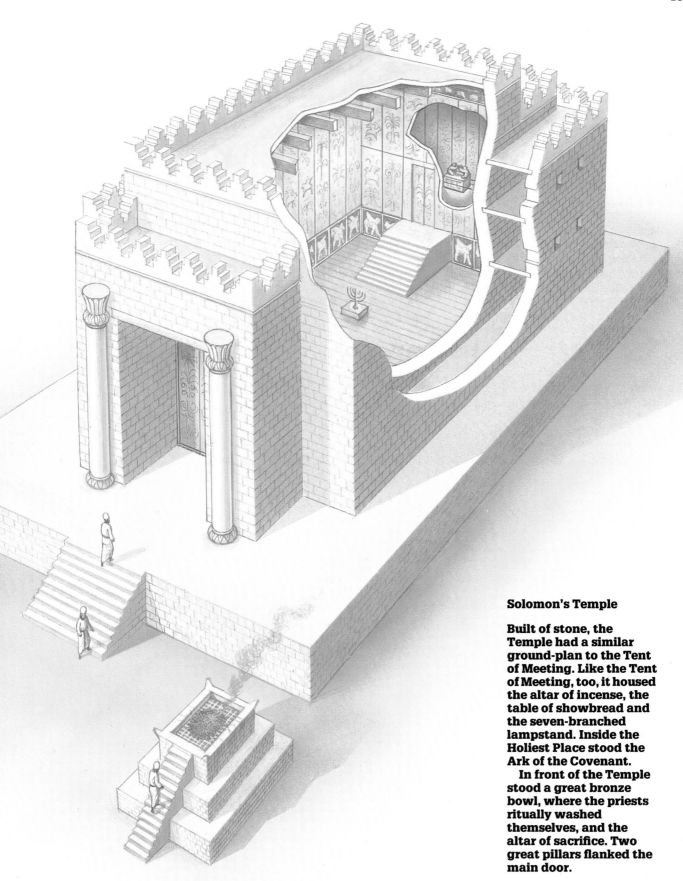

Solomon's Temple

Built of stone, the Temple had a similar ground-plan to the Tent of Meeting. Like the Tent of Meeting, too, it housed the altar of incense, the table of showbread and the seven-branched lampstand. Inside the Holiest Place stood the Ark of the Covenant.

In front of the Temple stood a great bronze bowl, where the priests ritually washed themselves, and the altar of sacrifice. Two great pillars flanked the main door.

Waging War

In Old Testament times, the Israelites were constantly involved in warfare, first to conquer the Promised Land, then to secure it from a succession of enemies and invaders. Like the modern state of Israel, the Israelites had always to be prepared to do battle.

Since God was involved in every aspect of Israel's life, the priests accompanied the armies of Israel into battle, and sometimes prophets were asked for guidance before a military campaign began.

Weapons

During the period of the Judges, the main weapons of the foot-soldier were the spear and axe, while the curved cutting-sword, with its single sharp edge, was improved by the lengthening of its blade. We cannot be certain what Israelite soldiers looked like, since it was forbidden to Israel to picture the human form.

Among other weapons used later by the Israelites were the sling, the javelin, the bow and arrow, and the huge battering-ram for attacking fortresses and cities under siege.

Military methods

On campaign, the army would use a variety of methods and strategies: ambushes, as in Joshua's attack on the city of Ai (Joshua 8); feinting movements; surprise attacks; raids; forays and many others. Sometimes, when opposing armies were drawn up, a champion from each side would be chosen to fight to decide the issue – as in the famous conflict between the young David and Goliath, champion of the Philistine army.

After a victory, the winning army would often raid the enemy camp, robbing the dead and killing or mutilating prisoners. When a city was under siege, the attacking army might well throw up great earthworks against the walls, and then use battering rams to pound away at the defences. The besieged population would try to defend itself by throwing darts and stones, and shooting arrows.

An Egyptian soldier.

A Philistine warrior.

An Assyrian spearman.

An Assyrian relief, showing an assault on a stronghold, using siege-engines and ladders.

The army

From the beginnings of the nation, every Israelite could be called on to fight. But it was not until the time of King Saul that a permanent army was formed, directly under the king's control. King David was the first ruler to have in addition a personal bodyguard of picked men.

For many years the Israelites were at a disadvantage in the face of their enemies, the Canaanites, the Philistines and the Egyptians, since these all had chariots, while the Israelites only had foot-soldiers. Solomon was the first ruler of Israel to use chariots, although they were not very practical for much of the hill-fighting at which the Israelites were so good.

A Greek warrior.

An Israelite archer.

A Babylonian foot-soldier.

Who's Who
in the Old Testament

Aaron 'enlightened'
Moses' brother, he became
the first high priest and
founder of the priesthood
of Israel. In the incident of
the golden calf, Aaron
gave way to the people's
demand for an idol.
Exodus 2, 4, 17, 32

Abel 'shepherd'
The second son of Adam
and Eve, Abel was a
shepherd, murdered by his
brother Cain.
Genesis 4

Abram or Abraham
Founder of the Jewish
nation, his name was
changed from Abram – 'the
father is exalted' – to
Abraham – 'father of
multitudes'. He left Ur,
eventually settling in
Canaan, where God
repeated his promise to
make him father of a great
nation; his barren wife,
Sarah, was given a son,
Isaac.
Genesis 11–25

Absalom 'father of peace'
David's third son, who
rebelled against his father,
driving him from

NOAH

Jerusalem. He was killed
in the war that followed.
2 Samuel 14, 19; 1 Kings 15

Adam 'mankind'
The first man, after whose
disobedience the whole
creation was altered, and
death entered the world.
Genesis 1, 2

Ahab 'uncle'
The seventh king of Israel,
a wicked idol-worshipper
who married the infamous
Jezebel.
1 Kings 16–22

JOSHUA

Amos 'burden-bearer'
A shepherd from Judah,
sent north to Israel to
prophesy during the reign
of Jeroboam.
Amos

Benjamin 'son of the right
hand'
Youngest son of Jacob and
Rachel, his descendants
became one of the twelve
tribes of Israel.
Genesis 35, 42–45

Daniel 'God is my judge'
Jewish prophet in Babylon
in the time of King
Nebuchadnezzar; his

REBEKAH

wisdom and ability to
interpret dreams brought
him a high position.
Daniel 1–2, 6

David 'beloved'
Son of Jesse, a Bethlehem
farmer, David became a
great statesman, general,
poet and king of Israel,
uniting the divided tribes
and preparing for the
rebuilding of the Temple.
*1 Samuel 16 – 1 Kings 2; 1
Chronicles 11–29*

Elijah 'Yahweh is my God'
A prophet during the reign
of King Ahab, Elijah led the
struggle against idolatrous
worship of Baal.
1 Kings 17 – 2 Kings 2

Elisha 'God is Saviour'
Elijah's successor as
prophet in Israel, Elisha
lived through the reigns of
six kings of Israel.
1 Kings 19; 2 Kings 2–9

Esau 'hairy'
Isaac's oldest son and
Jacob's twin brother, Esau
lost his rights as eldest son
to Jacob, and later founded
the tribe of Edom.
Genesis 25; 27–28; 32–33

Esther 'star'
A Jewish orphan who
became queen of Persia,
Esther saved her people
from extinction, a
deliverance remembered
in the annual festival of
Purim.
Esther

Eve 'life'
The first woman, and
Adam's companion. They
disobeyed God's
command not to eat of the
fruit of the tree.
Genesis 2–4

Ezekiel 'God strengthens'
Jewish prophet taken
captive to Babylon, where
he continued to prophesy
by the river Chebar.
Ezekiel 1, 3, 24

Ezra 'help'
Jewish priest and teacher
of the Law, he led a group
of Jews back from exile in
Babylon, and worked with
Nehemiah to re-establish
the Law.
Ezra 5 – 10; Nehemiah 8

MOSES

Gideon 'great warrior'
Judge of Israel who
defeated their great
enemy, the Midianites.
Judges 6 – 8

Haggai 'festive'
The first prophet to
prophesy after the
Babylonian Captivity.
Ezra 5; Haggai

Hezekiah 'Yahweh is
strength'
The twelfth king of Judah,

RUTH

Hezekiah re-opened the Temple and introduced religious reforms.
1 Kings 18–20; 2 Chronicles 29–32

Hosea 'Yahweh is help'
A prophet of Israel, he denounced idolatry in Israel and Samaria.
Hosea

Isaac 'laughter'
The son of Abraham and Sarah in their old age, the husband of Rebekah, and father of Esau and Jacob.
Genesis 21–26

Isaiah 'salvation of Yahweh'
Major Jewish prophet living in Jerusalem from the time of King Uzziah to the time of King Hezekiah. His prophecies are frequently quoted in the New Testament in connection with their fulfilment.
2 Kings 19–20; Isaiah 1

DAVID

Jacob 'supplanter'
Son of Isaac and Rebekah, and Esau's younger twin, Jacob bought Esau's birthright and became father of the Jewish nation. His name was changed to 'Israel' ('God strives').
Genesis 25–50

Jeremiah 'Yahweh is high'
Prophet during the reigns of the last five kings of Judah, Jeremiah was unpopular because of his message of doom for the nation.
Jeremiah 1–2, 36

Job 'persecuted'
A pious man, Job was tested when he lost all.
Job

SAUL

Jonah 'dove'
A Hebrew prophet sent to denounce the city of Nineveh, Jonah was the first prophet sent to a heathen nation. He fled to sea instead; God rescued him from the water by means of a great fish.
Jonah

Joseph 'increaser'
A son of Jacob and Rachel, Joseph was sold into slavery by his brothers, but became second to the pharaoh of Egypt, and was later able to save his people from famine.
Genesis 37–50

Joshua 'Yahweh is salvation'
Moses' successor, Joshua led the Israelites to conquer the Promised Land, and divided it among the twelve tribes.
Exodus 17; Deuteronomy 31, 34

SOLOMON

Malachi 'messenger of Yahweh'
Prophet of the time of Nehemiah; his book comes last in the Old Testament.
Malachi

Moses 'drawer out'
The great leader and lawgiver of Israel, brought up in the Egyptian court, Moses led his people from slavery in Egypt to the edge of the Promised Land.
Exodus 2 – Deuteronomy 34

Noah 'rest'
A pious man in an evil age, Noah built the ark that saved his family and the animals from the Flood.
Genesis 5 – 10

Rebekah 'flattering'
The wife of Isaac and mother of Jacob and Esau.
Genesis 22, 24–28

Ruth 'companion'
A Moabitess who returned to Bethlehem with her mother-in-law, Naomi, when her husband died, Ruth married Boaz, an ancestor of David.
Ruth

Samuel 'asked of God'
The last great judge of Israel and one of the first prophets, Samuel anointed Saul as Israel's first king and, later, David.
1 Samuel 3 – 16; 19

Saul 'asked'
The first king of Israel, Saul later turned from God and tried several times to kill David. He died in battle at Gilboa.
1 Samuel 9 – 31

Solomon 'peace'
The son of David by Bathsheba, Solomon was king of a united and strong Israel for forty years. Renowned for his riches and wisdom, he built the first Temple in Jerusalem.
1 Kings 1 – 11

Zechariah 'Yahweh my righteousness'
A prophet during the time of Ezra.
Ezra 5; Zechariah

The New Testament

Like the Old Testament, the New Testament is made up of a number of different, shorter books – a total of twenty-seven in all. And, also like the Old Testament, the books of the New Testament can be divided into several types:

1. **History** – the first five books, which include the four Gospels and the book of Acts, Luke's account of the early years of the church.

2. **Letters** – both letters from the Apostle Paul, such as Romans, Galatians and Philemon, and other letters, such as the letter to the Hebrews and the letters of Peter and James.

3. **The Revelation of John** – a book of letters to seven churches in Asia Minor (modern Turkey) including John's visions concerning the last days.

The World of the New Testament

Throughout New Testament times, the Romans had overall control of the country of Palestine. They ruled through their own governors and through the Herod family.

At the time of Jesus' birth, Herod the Great was still king, and was greatly trusted by the Romans. When he died, in 4 BC, his cruel son Archelaus succeeded him as ruler of Judea, but was soon removed by the Romans. Herod's son Antipas became ruler of Galilee and the region of Perea; it was he who executed John the Baptist. A third son of Herod, Philip, ruled the regions of Iturea and Trachonitis, north-east of the Sea of Galilee; his capital was Caesarea Philippi.

After the exile of Archelaus, the Romans ruled Judea directly through officials called 'procurators'. These men lived in Caesarea on the Mediterranean coast, and only came up to Jerusalem for special occasions, such as the great religious festivals. The best known of these procurators was Pontius Pilate, who was in Jerusalem for the Passover when Jesus was brought before him for trial and sentencing to death.

Herod Agrippa I rose to power between AD 37–44, and took over from the Roman procurators. He gained in popularity with the Jews by his policy of persecuting the Christians.

After his sudden death in AD 44, Roman procurators ruled once more, but their insensitive harshness finally provoked the Jewish rebellion of 66 – 70, which resulted in the destruction of the Holy City of Jerusalem and the razing to the ground of Herod's Temple. Among the later Roman procurators were Felix (52–60) and Festus (62–64), both of whom met the apostle Paul.

History

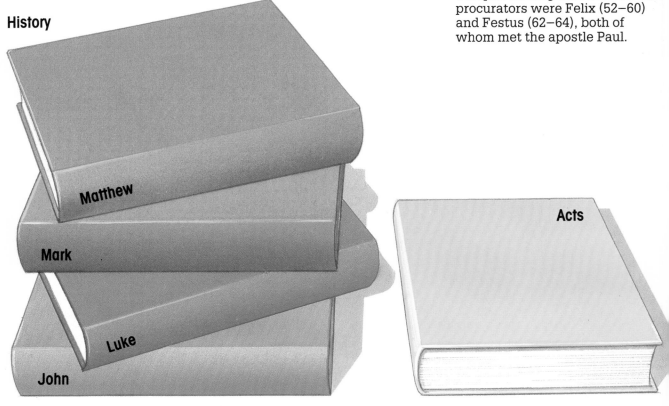

Matthew

Mark

Luke

John

Acts

so that what they say is what he wants to say to us. It is important, therefore, that we read the Bible in the right way.

Listening to God

We can read the Bible for information – about ancient times, about God and about human need and ideals. We can read the Bible for enjoyment, for much of it is not only well written but also contains gripping accounts of incidents strong in human interest. Christians will, above all else, want to read the Bible in order to hear God and to develop a growing relationship with him. They will ask God to help them understand, and when they hear they will be prepared to act in response.

Hearing God

Because writers of the Bible wrote in times very different from ours, it is not always easy to understand their message. We need to know something of the background to their books. There are different types of writing – poetry, prophecy, Gospels and letters, for instance – and knowing this will help us to understand what might otherwise be strange expressions.

First of all we must discover what it was that God through the writer was saying to the first readers; then we ask how that message applies in our day.

How to start

There are many ways to read the Bible. We can read right through a book – Mark's Gospel might be a good place to start. Or we may choose to look at the life of one person, or follow a particular theme.

Christians read the Bible to hear God speaking to them.

Reading the Bible

The Bible contains many books, written at different times and by different authors.

Yet they have one common aim, for the Bible is more than a collection of human books. It is God's message to us, and he guided and instructed each of the writers

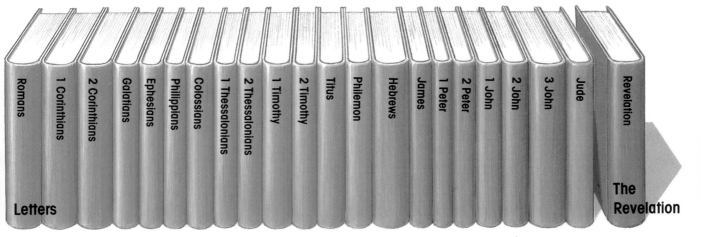

Letters: Romans, 1 Corinthians, 2 Corinthians, Galatians, Ephesians, Philippians, Colossians, 1 Thessalonians, 2 Thessalonians, 1 Timothy, 2 Timothy, Titus, Philemon, Hebrews, James, 1 Peter, 2 Peter, 1 John, 2 John, 3 John, Jude

The Revelation

The Land

Jesus preached his message in a particular place at a particular time: Palestine during the Roman occupation. It is important to look closely at the landscape of Palestine and its various regions.

The present landscape of Palestine was formed in very distant times when the rocky platform of the land was broken, and a long, deep trough – the Jordan Valley – was created. This geological fault made a valley about 480 kilometres (300 miles) long, 48 kilometres (30 miles) wide and 1000 metres (3000 feet) deep.

This movement of the land created the five main geographical regions in Palestine.

The Plains
A narrow coastal strip, which sweeps inland near Mount Tabor to form the great Valley of Esdraelon, or Jezreel.

The Hill Country
The hills and valleys that make up the area between the plains and the Jordan Rift Valley. The slopes can be cultivated.

The Desert
A barren wilderness stretching southwards from the Dead Sea.

The Jordan Valley
The rift valley described above, which contains the Sea of Galilee and the Dead Sea. The latter has no outlet, and, since water cannot escape except by evaporation, it is very rich in salt.

The Trans-Jordan Mountains
A high platform of land, partly fertile, partly barren.

Top: Mount Hermon marked the northern border of Israel. **Above:** Part of the hill-country. **Above right:** A view of the Valley of Esdraelon, from Megiddo. **Right:** Tiberias and the Sea of Galilee.

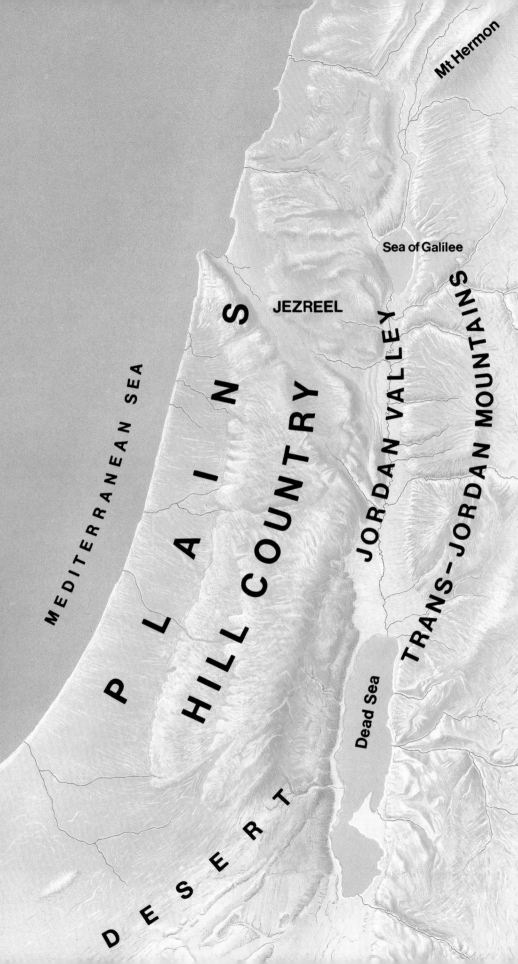

Mt Hermon

Sea of Galilee

JEZREEL

MEDITERRANEAN SEA

P L A I N S

HILL COUNTRY

JORDAN VALLEY

TRANS–JORDAN MOUNTAINS

Dead Sea

D E S E R T

The Home

Ordinary people's houses were very simple in design and construction. They were built of mud, or lath and plaster, and normally consisted of just one main room. Houses had flat roofs where people could rest, sleep or work, and would sometimes be covered by an awning. The roof would be made of brushwood, clay and earth, and had to be kept flat with a special roller.

The roof was reached by means of a flight of steps up the outside wall of the house. By law, every house had to have a parapet around the edge of the roof to prevent people falling off. The roof was the scene of much activity: people would talk there, go there to meditate and pray, and also use it for drying linen, flax, figs and other fruit.

A house at Chorazin, partly rebuilt to show how it looked originally.

Inside the home

Inside, the house was divided into living and sleeping areas for animals and humans. The floor would be of beaten mud, though sometimes the family would live on a slightly raised platform area. Windows were small, high and few in number, to keep the building as cool as possible in the sun's heat; windows were not glazed, but sometimes had a latticed covering.

The dark room would be lit with little oil lamps, sometimes supported on a tripod or on an upturned pot. The door of the house would be very low – people had to stoop to enter.

The woman of the house was responsible for household work – cleaning, cooking, spinning, weaving, sewing. She also occasionally helped in the fields and vineyards and taught her children in their earliest years.

Furniture

There would be very little furniture in the ordinary peasant's home. At night the family would unroll coarse skins to sleep on and would simply take off their sandals and belts when they lay down to sleep.

A peasant woman bakes bread in a simple oven.

A woman grinds grain to make flour for cooking.

There were probably two main meals each day – a light breakfast and a more substantial supper in the evening. Breakfast would consist of bread, fruits and cheese; supper of meat, vegetables and wine. The poorer people normally sat on the floor to eat.

Baking was normally done by the woman of the house, and fresh bread made every day. After grinding the grain, she would make the dough, knead it, and bake it either in an oven or over the hearth. Smoke from the hearth escaped through cracks in the roof and walls; there was no chimney.

Two women work in the fields, breaking up the soil.

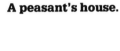

A peasant's house.

Education

Until New Testament times, children were usually educated informally by their parents. Only religious leaders would learn to read and write; for the rest, practical skills for running the home and working the land were more important.

During a child's first years, the mother was largely reponsible for his or her upbringing. But once a boy was old enough, he was set to work alongside his father, to begin learning the skills of his craft or trade. It was the mother's job to train her daughters in the skills needed to make a good wife and mother.

It was the parents, too, who brought up their children to know the history of the Jewish people and God's dealings with them. The children would memorize passages that summed up Israel's history as God's people. At religious festivals such as Passover, the father would take the opportunity to explain the meaning of the feast to his children – and especially to his sons.

A Babylonian tablet. It includes the story of the fall of Nineveh.

Writing

As we have seen, the Old Testament was originally written in Hebrew. The Hebrew language has an alphabet of twenty-two consonants – but no written vowels. Instead of reading left to right, Hebrew is read right to left.

The New Testament was originally written in *Koine* Greek, a language with twenty-four letters in its alphabet.

In Bible times, people did not write on paper but on various other materials, such as clay tablets, pieces of pots, waxed boards, and pieces of wood. They also wrote on parchment, made from sheep-skin, leather, and papyrus, a sort of paper made from the papyrus reed which grew in the swamps around the river Nile. A sharp-pointed stylus was used to write on wax or wood, and a reed brush or quill pen on papyrus and parchment.

In Old Testament times, pages of writing were usually joined up length-ways, and then rolled up to make a continuous scroll. By New Testament times, people had started to make books by sewing pages together at the edges.

In ancient times, stone tablets and multi-sided stones (top) were sometimes used for making official records. People also used wooden writing boards with waxed writing surfaces (bottom right), and sometimes wrote direct onto wooden boards (left).

School was open all the year round, but lasted only four hours each day. The boys attended class during the cooler parts of the day, before ten in the morning and after three in the afternoon. The teacher would sit on a little platform with a rack of scrolls of Scripture in front of him. The boys at his feet would often recite aloud to learn passages of the Scriptures by heart. Boys were expected to know Jewish history and the Law thoroughly and to be able to read, write and do arithmetic.

Teachers

After the Jews returned from exile in Babylon, a special sort of Bible scholar called a 'scribe' arose. The scribes were men who could write, and sometimes offered their services to people who were illiterate. But they were, more importantly, men who were learned in the Law. They became famous as 'rabbis' or 'lawyers' – men who explained the Law of God to the people. In time, their sayings were collected and written down in special books, called the *Mishnah*.

The synagogue at Capernaum. This building probably dates from after the time of Jesus.

The synagogue school

By Jesus' time, however, synagogue schools had become a vital part of Jewish life. During the week, the boys would go to classes to study the Scriptures. From about the age of six or seven, the younger boys would meet at the teacher's house, reading short passages of Scripture.

The older boys met at the synagogue itself, where they were taught by the keeper of the scrolls of the Law in the room where the scrolls were kept. Later still, they would progress to discussing the Law with the Pharisee teachers.

A teacher with his class of young boys.

Jesus in Galilee

The church at Tabgha.

Kursi (Gerasa).

The Sea of Galilee.

The synagogue, Chorazin.

Jesus spent much of his ministry preaching and healing in Galilee. This was a Jewish province, but many non-Jews also settled here. The Galileans had a dialect of their own, and were despised by many of the Jews in Jerusalem.

In Jesus' time there were many towns around the shores of the Sea of Galilee, which is also known as the Lake of Gennesareth, the Sea of Tiberias and the Sea of Chinnereth. It was while sailing across the lake with his disciples that Jesus calmed a sudden storm (Mark 4:35–41).

Jesus also visited Bethsaida, where he restored the sight of a blind man (Mark 8:22), and withdrew for a time of rest (Luke 9:10). At Magdala, Jesus dined with Simon the Pharisee, when Mary anointed him (Luke 7:36–8:2).

Capernaum
Jesus came to live here (Matthew 4:13) and cured a Roman officer's slave (Matthew 8:5–12), a leper (Matthew 8:2–3), Peter's mother-in-law (Matthew 8:14–15), a man with an evil spirit (Mark 1:21–26), and a paralyzed man (Mark 2:1–12). Jesus preached in the Capernaum synagogue (John 6), called Matthew (Matthew 9:9), paid the Temple tax here (Matthew 17:24), and denounced the town for its lack of faith (Matthew 11:23).

Chorazin
Jesus performed miracles here, and later denounced the people for their lack of faith (Matthew 11:21; Luke 10:13).

Tabgha
This may be the place where the risen Christ met his apostles and ate with them (John 21).

Land of the Gerasenes
Jesus cured the man with evil spirits near here (Mark 5:1–20).

Mount of the Beatitudes
By tradition the hill where Jesus taught the Beatitudes (Matthew 5:1–12).

This church stands on the hill where it is believed Jesus gave the Sermon on the Mount.

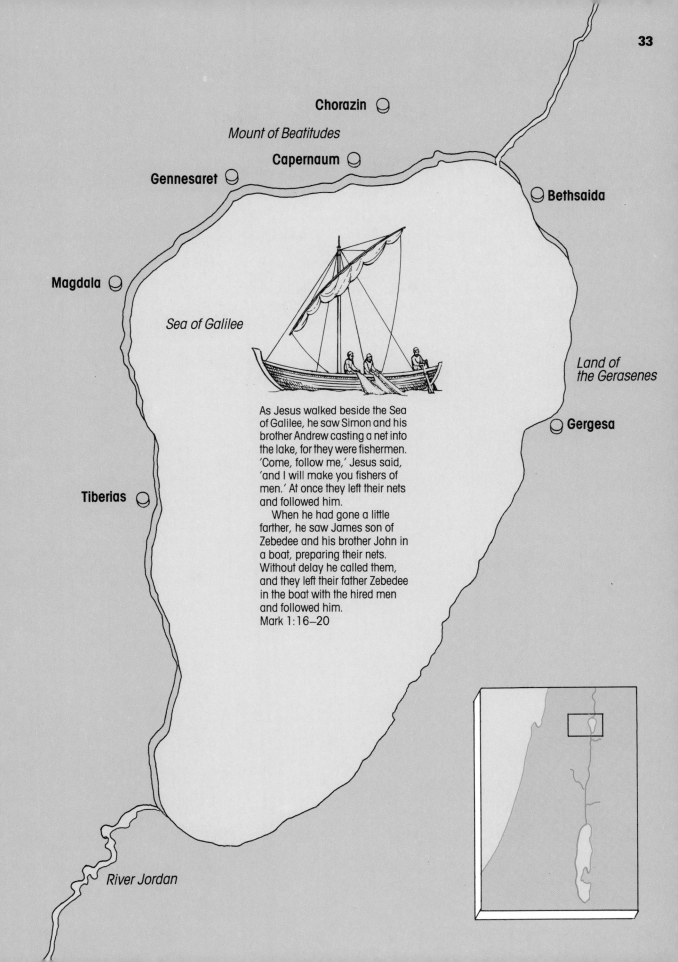

Chorazin

Mount of Beatitudes

Capernaum

Gennesaret

Bethsaida

Magdala

Sea of Galilee

Land of
the Gerasenes

Gergesa

As Jesus walked beside the Sea
of Galilee, he saw Simon and his
brother Andrew casting a net into
the lake, for they were fishermen.
'Come, follow me,' Jesus said,
'and I will make you fishers of
men.' At once they left their nets
and followed him.

When he had gone a little
farther, he saw James son of
Zebedee and his brother John in
a boat, preparing their nets.
Without delay he called them,
and they left their father Zebedee
in the boat with the hired men
and followed him.
Mark 1:16–20

Tiberias

River Jordan

Work

Farming was, of course, the most important occupation in Bible times, and we have looked at the farmer's year earlier. However, unlike today, when we have specialists to do most jobs, in Bible times most day-to-day tasks were done by the family. They would often own their plot of land, farm it, raise a few sheep and goats, do their own spinning, weaving, clothes-making, food preparation and cooking. The men did the heavier jobs such as building construction.

But there were still a number of specialist crafts and trades; for instance, casting metal vessels, carpentry, linen-making, pottery, gold-smithing, perfume manufacture and others.

By New Testament times, with the growth of large towns, there were yet more specialist trades, such as bakers, sandal makers, builders, tailors, nail makers, tanners, tax collectors and weavers. In New Testament Jerusalem we know there was a separate smith's market, so noisy that it had to be closed down during some religious festivals.

Leather working too was an important trade; leather was needed to make clothes, foot-wear, belts, wine- and water-bottles, and even as a writing material.

Fishing
Only in New Testament times did fishing become an important trade; a lively fishing industry had grown up on the Sea of Galilee, as we know from the Gospels. Fishermen used either hand-nets cast from the land, or large drag-nets, often towed behind two fishing boats.

Medicine
Health was not neglected; the rabbis insisted that each town have its own physician and, if possible, a surgeon too. The Temple officials always included a doctor, whose job it was to look after the Temple priests.

In New Testament times, Greek and Roman medicine probably began to influence Jewish practice. Luke, the Gospel writer, was trained as a doctor, and often uses medical phrases in Luke and Acts.

The carpenter
The carpenter was much needed in Bible times for making all sorts of things from simple household furniture to chariots and carts. He also found work making doors, panels and beams for great buildings such as the Temple in Jerusalem. Because wood became scarce in Israel, it was often imported from abroad,

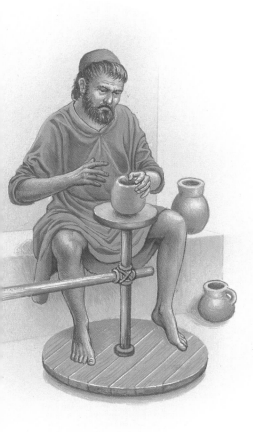

A potter at his wheel.

A fisherman on shore mends his nets while others at sea pull in their catch.

Fish are still plentiful in the Sea of Galilee.

A woman weaves at her upright loom.

particularly from Lebanon and Nubia.

The carpenter's tools included the saw, chisel, set-square, hammer, drill, pincers and plane, as well as a plumb-line, for making sure what he made was upright, an adze, for stripping wood, and an awl, for making small holes in the wood.

The potter

Because so many pots and bowls were made of clay, the potter was vital. He could use three different methods of working the clay:
1. He could press the clay into a mould, for example to make an oil lamp.
2. He could mould the clay with his fingers.
3. He could use a wheel on which the clay was shaped while he kept it spinning round.

After it was finished, the pot or bowl was fired in a heated kiln to harden it for use.

Most eating and drinking vessels were made of pottery, as were oil-lamps, grain, wine and water containers, perfume jars, and even toys. The Israelites tended to make fairly plain pots, and, in Jesus' time, high-quality pottery was often imported from other parts of the Roman Empire.

Carpenters' tools have altered little over the centuries.

Jesus' Last Week in Jerusalem

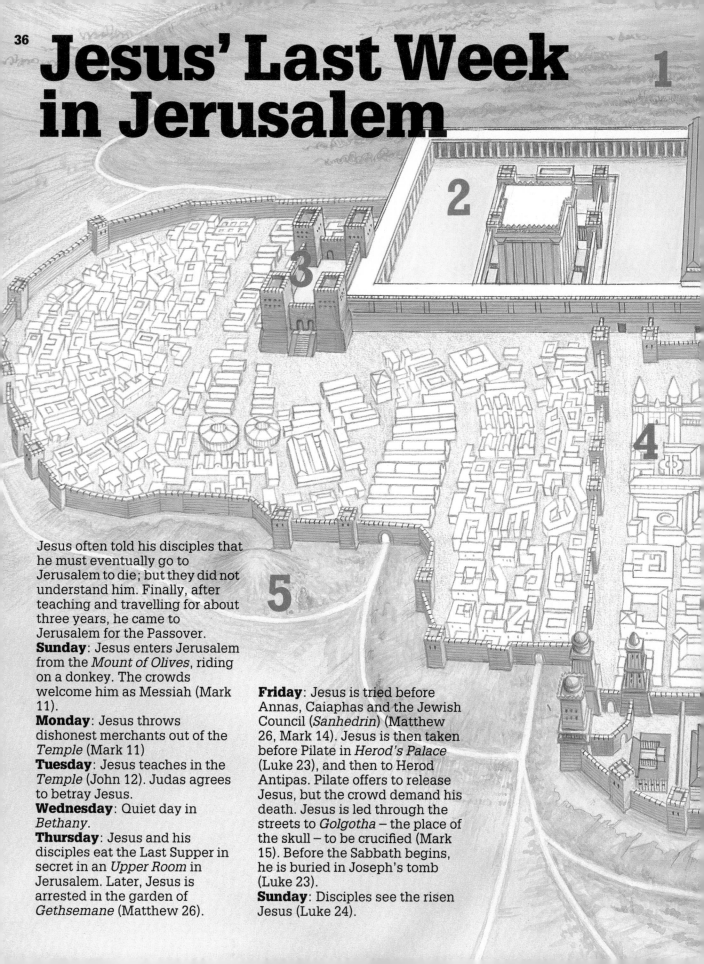

Jesus often told his disciples that he must eventually go to Jerusalem to die; but they did not understand him. Finally, after teaching and travelling for about three years, he came to Jerusalem for the Passover.

Sunday: Jesus enters Jerusalem from the *Mount of Olives*, riding on a donkey. The crowds welcome him as Messiah (Mark 11).

Monday: Jesus throws dishonest merchants out of the *Temple* (Mark 11)

Tuesday: Jesus teaches in the *Temple* (John 12). Judas agrees to betray Jesus.

Wednesday: Quiet day in *Bethany*.

Thursday: Jesus and his disciples eat the Last Supper in secret in an *Upper Room* in Jerusalem. Later, Jesus is arrested in the garden of *Gethsemane* (Matthew 26).

Friday: Jesus is tried before Annas, Caiaphas and the Jewish Council (*Sanhedrin*) (Matthew 26, Mark 14). Jesus is then taken before Pilate in *Herod's Palace* (Luke 23), and then to Herod Antipas. Pilate offers to release Jesus, but the crowd demand his death. Jesus is led through the streets to *Golgotha* – the place of the skull – to be crucified (Mark 15). Before the Sabbath begins, he is buried in Joseph's tomb (Luke 23).

Sunday: Disciples see the risen Jesus (Luke 24).

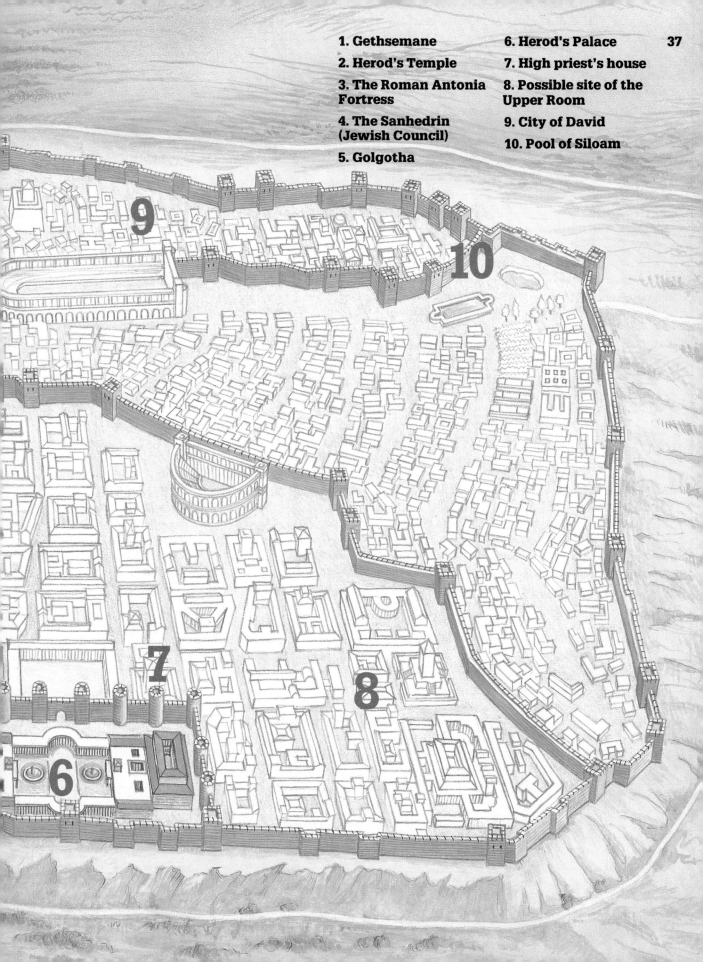

1. Gethsemane
2. Herod's Temple
3. The Roman Antonia Fortress
4. The Sanhedrin (Jewish Council)
5. Golgotha
6. Herod's Palace
7. High priest's house
8. Possible site of the Upper Room
9. City of David
10. Pool of Siloam

The Good News Spreads

MEDITERRANEAN SEA

to Cyprus

After the coming of the Holy Spirit, the believers in Jerusalem found a new strength; they began to preach boldly, and increased in numbers daily. They were not long ignored by the Jewish authorities, who tried to stop the young movement, but, in doing so, helped it spread.

to Damascus

Some believers fled to Damascus. When Paul arrived there, after his conversion, he found Christians there already (Acts 9).

Remains of the Roman harbour, Caesarea.

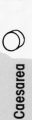
Caesarea

Roman columns at Samaria. Samaria

Peter went to Caesarea, where he stayed with Simon the tanner, and restored Tabitha to life. He was shown in a vision that he should take the gospel to the officer Cornelius, a Roman.

River Jordan

Dead Sea

Jerusalem

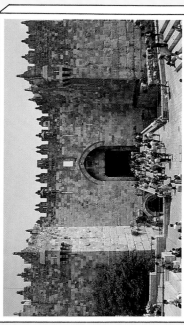

The Damascus Gate, Jerusalem.

Peter, John and Philip all travelled to Samaria to preach the good news there.

The beach, Jaffa – biblical Joppa.

Stephen was one of the leaders of the church in Jerusalem; but the Jews accused him of blasphemy and had him stoned to death (Acts 6–7). After his martyrdom, believers in Jerusalem were persecuted, and many escaped – south into Judea, north to Samaria, and west to the coast and even to Cyprus.

Philip set out from Jerusalem to Gaza. On his way he met the treasurer of the queen of Ethiopia. Philip explained the gospel to him and baptized him, before going on to preach at the Mediterranean coast towns.

Joppa

Travel

Land travel

We often read of journeys in the Bible; in Genesis, Abraham's great journey from Ur to Canaan; in the book of Acts, Paul's epic missionary travels.

Most people normally travelled on foot in Bible times. The roads were often very stony and uneven, and in the desert the way would be marked by large stones placed at intervals. Travel was therefore slow; it would take a walker at least three days to cover the seventy miles between Galilee and Jerusalem.

For carrying packs, people generally used asses or mules. The ass was cheaper to feed than the horse and could carry much heavier loads. Camels had to be used for crossing the waterless deserts, since they can cover long distances without needing to drink.

Israel formed a kind of 'bridge' between Europe and Asia in the north and Africa in the south, and major roads ran across the country. When travelling long distances, merchants often formed themselves into groups, or caravans, of asses and camels, hoping that their large numbers would deter brigands.

In Old Testament times, horse-drawn chariots were used in battle, though they would often get stuck in rougher country. By New Testament times, many of the wealthier people also had horses to draw their chariots; in town they would sometimes also be carried about in a litter – a kind of portable couch resting on poles and carried by horses or slaves. By contrast, the farmer usually used cattle or asses to pull his farm carts.

When the Romans occupied Israel, they built good roads on which their legions and chariots could travel safely and rapidly.

Sea travel

Sea travel was very dangerous in Bible times. It was safe to cross the Mediterranean Sea only in summer. The Israelites knew little about seafaring, and King Solomon was the only Old Testament ruler to build a navy for Israel. During his successful reign, Israel exported iron and copper, and imported luxury goods such as precious stones and fine timber, often by sea.

When Jesus sailed across the Sea of Galilee, it was probably in one of the little fishing-boats based on the lake. Fishing became important in Palestine only in New Testament times.

During his sea travels, the apostle Paul usually sailed in Roman ships. On his final journey to Rome we know he went in a grain ship carrying 276 people. (There is a detailed description of his voyage in Acts 27.) Roman grain ships could be as long as 60 metres (200 feet).

A harbour scene in New Testament times. On the quay are (**left to right**) a Roman charioteer, a peasant with his donkey, and a litter carried by slaves. A small fishing boat is tying up at the quay, and a Roman grain ship lies further out to sea.

imported from abroad. They also imported exotic creatures such as monkeys and peacocks.

In New Testament times, Israel imported a variety of goods, such as cotton and silk from the east, glass bowls from Tyre and Sidon, apples from Crete, cheese from Bithynia, fish from Spain, wine from Italy and beer from Media. The country exported much olive oil to Egypt. Merchants were regarded as important men in Israel; even priests took part in trading.

A relief showing a Greek horse-drawn chariot.

Trade

In Old Testament times, Israel exported agricultural crops and other produce, such as fruit, nuts, honey, oil and grain, along with wool, woollen cloth, and clothes made by Israelite weavers. In return, Israel imported metals such as lead, copper, tin and silver, as well as wood from Lebanon, and linen from Egypt and Syria.

Wealthy Israelites bought gems, gold, silver and spices

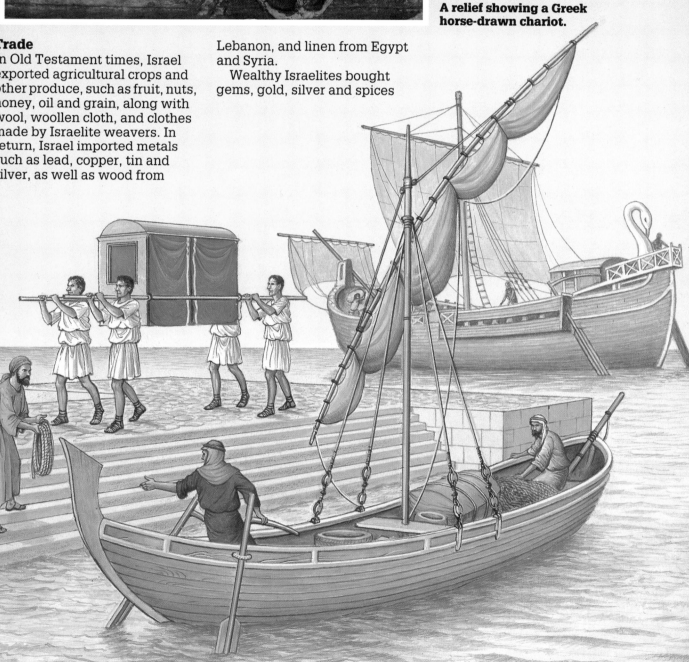

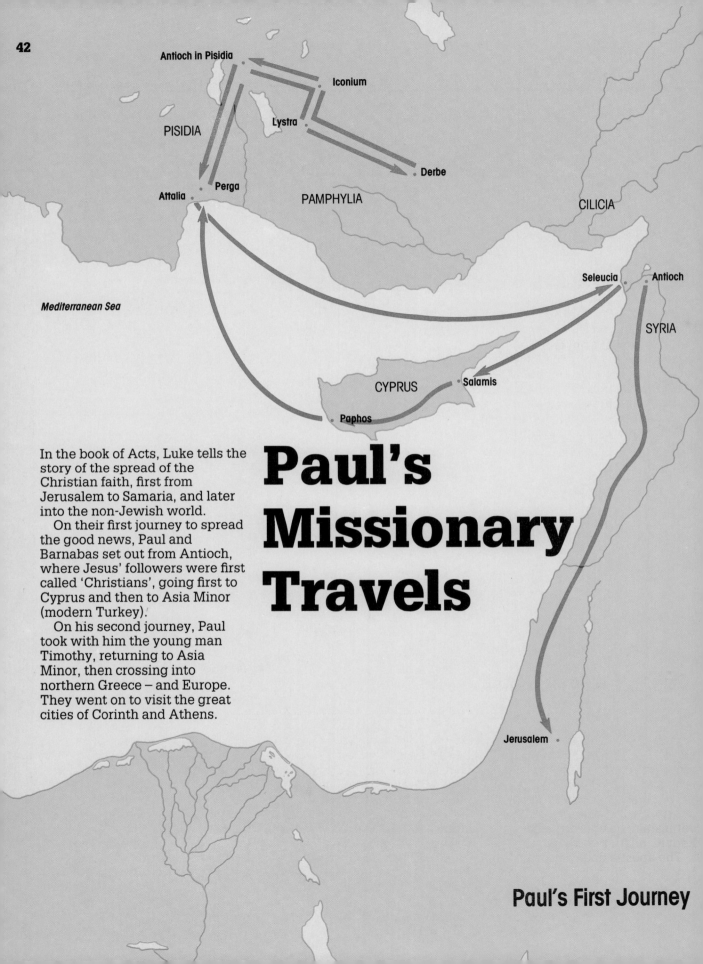

Antioch in Pisidia

Iconium

Lystra

PISIDIA

Derbe

Attalia   Perga

PAMPHYLIA

CILICIA

Mediterranean Sea

Seleucia   Antioch

SYRIA

CYPRUS   Salamis

Paphos

Paul's Missionary Travels

In the book of Acts, Luke tells the
story of the spread of the
Christian faith, first from
Jerusalem to Samaria, and later
into the non-Jewish world.

On their first journey to spread
the good news, Paul and
Barnabas set out from Antioch,
where Jesus' followers were first
called 'Christians', going first to
Cyprus and then to Asia Minor
(modern Turkey).

On his second journey, Paul
took with him the young man
Timothy, returning to Asia
Minor, then crossing into
northern Greece – and Europe.
They went on to visit the great
cities of Corinth and Athens.

Jerusalem

Paul's First Journey

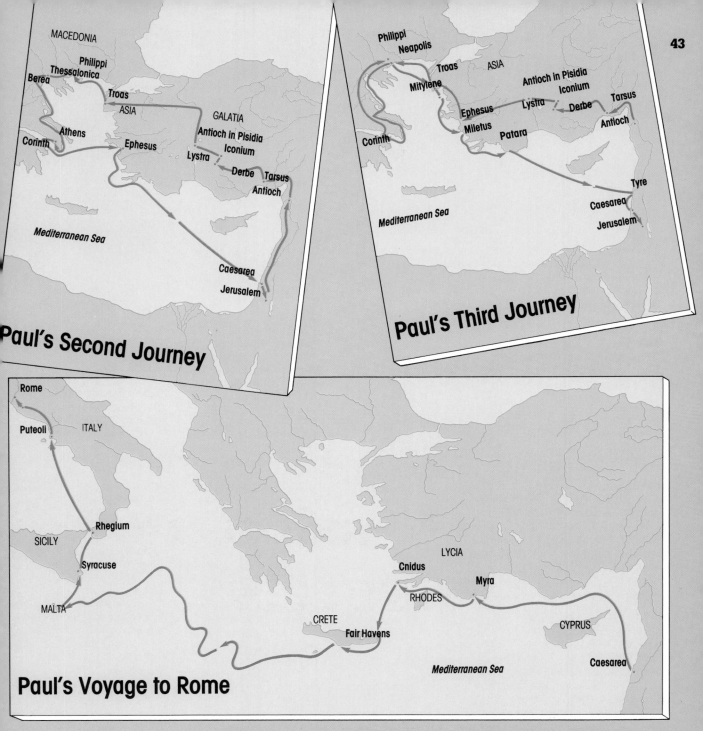

Paul's Second Journey

Paul's Third Journey

Paul's Voyage to Rome

During his third journey, Paul stayed in Ephesus for two years, working and teaching, and also revisited many of his previous ports of call, to consolidate his previous work. Returning to Jerusalem, he was arrested and kept in jail for two years.

The apostle finally appealed his case to Caesar, and was sent to Rome for trial, where it is believed he met his death by execution some years later.

Paul was far from impressive to look at; he is described as 'a short man, with a bald head and crooked legs; his body is fit and healthy; his eyebrows meet over his nose, which is rather hooked; his face is full of friendliness'. But he had great gifts in reaching people with the good news of Jesus Christ.

With his Jewish upbringing, he could argue for the faith from the Old Testament; with his Greek

culture, he could reach the non-Jewish people; and, with his Roman citizenship, he had the freedom to travel the empire.

But Paul rarely had things easy; time and again he suffered for the faith, being beaten, imprisoned, shipwrecked and finally executed. Despite the hardships, he worked tirelessly, taking the gospel to new places, and often returning to strengthen new believers in their faith.

Who's Who
in the New Testament

JUDAS ISCARIOT

HEROD THE GREAT

Andrew
The fisherman brother of Peter, and one of the twelve apostles.
Matthew 4, 10; John 1, 6; Acts 1

Aquila
A tentmaker and Jewish Christian friend of Paul.
Acts 18

Barabbas
Murderer who was released by Pontius Pilate instead of Jesus.
Matthew 27; Mark 15

Barnabas
Nickname, meaning 'son of encouragement', for Joses, a Jewish Christian from Cyprus, who travelled widely with Paul.
Acts 4, 9, 11, 12, 15

Caiaphas
The high priest in Jerusalem who found Jesus guilty of blasphemy and sent him to Pilate for sentence.
Matthew 26; John 11

Cleopas
One of the disciples who met the risen Christ on the Emmaus road.
Luke 24

Cornelius
A Roman centurion, stationed at Caesarea, who was converted to Christianity.
Acts 10

Elizabeth
Wife of the priest Zechariah, and mother, in old age, of John the Baptist.
Luke 1

Herod the Great
King of Judea at the time of Christ's birth, Herod ordered the killing of male children to eliminate any rival.
Matthew 2; Luke 1

Herod the Tetrarch
Son of Herod the Great, he imprisoned, and later beheaded, John the Baptist. Pilate sent Jesus to him for trial, since Jesus came from Galilee, Herod's territory.
Matthew 14; Luke 13, 23

James
Brother of Jesus, who, after Jesus' resurrection, became a leader of the Jerusalem church. He is possibly the writer of the letter of James.
Matthew 13; Acts 12; James

James
Fisherman son of Zebedee and brother of John, called by Jesus as one of his twelve apostles. James was present at Jesus' transfiguration, and was later put to death by Herod Agrippa I.
Matthew 4; Mark 5; Luke 9; Acts 12

John
Fisherman son of Zebedee, brother of James, and one of the twelve apostles, John, too, was present at the transfiguration. He is almost certainly 'the disciple whom Jesus loved', and whom Jesus told to care for his mother, Mary, after Jesus' death. Traditionally the author of John's Gospel, 1, 2 and 3 John, and the Revelation.
Matthew 4, 10, 17; John 19; Acts 3–4; Revelation 1

John the Baptist
Son of Elizabeth and Zechariah, John was sent by God to prepare the way for Jesus, the Messiah, preaching repentance and baptism. He was later imprisoned and beheaded by Herod the Tetrarch.
Matthew 3, 11, 14; Luke 1, 3, 7

JOSEPH

Joseph
Husband of Mary, the mother of Jesus. A Nazareth carpenter.
Matthew 1, 2; Luke 1, 2

Judas Iscariot
One of the twelve apostles, Judas betrayed Jesus and later hanged himself. Iscariot means 'man from Kerioth', a town near Hebron.
Matthew 10, 26, 27; John 12, 13.

Lazarus
The brother of Mary and Martha, Lazarus lived in Bethany and was raised from the dead by Jesus.
John 11

Luke
Greek-speaking doctor who accompanied Paul on some of his travels, and who wrote the Gospel of Luke and the Acts of the Apostles.
Colossians 4; 2 Timothy 4; Philemon

Mark (John Mark)
Son of Mary, in whose Jerusalem house the first Christians met; he went part-way with Paul on his first missionary journey, and wrote Mark's Gospel.
Mark 14; Acts 12, 15

Martha
The sister of Mary and Lazarus, Martha lived with them in Bethany.
Luke 10; John 11

Mary

Jesus' mother, whose song of faith, *The Magnificat*, is found in Luke 1. When he was dying on the cross, Jesus asked John to look after her.
Matthew 1; Luke 1–2; John 2, 19; Acts 1

Mary

The sister of Martha, Mary anointed Jesus with oil just before his death.
Luke 10; John 11

Mary Magdalene

From Magdala in Galilee, she was healed by Jesus. Later, she was the first to meet the risen Christ.
Matthew 27; Luke 8; John 19–20

MARY

Matthew

Also known as Levi, Matthew was one of the twelve apostles. He was a tax collector before his call, and is the author of the first Gospel.
Matthew 9–10; Mark 2; Luke 5

MARY MAGDALENE

PAUL

Nicodemus

A Pharisee and ruler of the Jews, Nicodemus came to talk to Jesus secretly by night, and later assisted at his burial.
John 3, 7, 19

Paul

Born in Tarsus and trained as a Pharisee, Paul was converted suddenly and became the apostle to the Gentiles. He made three great missionary journeys, founding and strengthening Christian churches wherever he went, and writing letters to encourage the believers. Paul was executed in Rome by Nero about AD 67.
Acts 7–28; Paul's letters: Romans – Philemon

Peter (Simon Peter)

A fisherman called to be an apostle, Peter was present at Jesus' transfiguration. The risen Christ appeared especially to Peter, who became one of the leaders of the early church, and was, by tradition, executed in Rome. He wrote two New Testament letters.
Matthew 4, 16–17; Acts 1–15; 1 and 2 Peter

Philip

One of the twelve apostles, Philip came from Bethsaida in Galilee.
Matthew 10; John 1, 6

Philip the evangelist

One of the seven men chosen to help the apostles in Jerusalem, Philip preached widely in Palestine.
Acts 6, 8

Pontius Pilate

Roman procurator of Judea. When Jesus was brought to him for trial, Pilate, afraid of the Jews, had him crucified, though he knew Jesus was innocent.
Matthew 27; John 18

Priscilla

Wife of Aquila; a faithful Jewish Christian and friend of Paul.
Acts 18

Silas

Silas was a leader of the Jerusalem church, and went with Paul on his second missionary journey.
Acts 15, 32–34; 2 Corinthians 1; 1 Thessalonians 1

PONTIUS PILATE

Stephen

A Greek-speaking Jew and one of the seven men chosen to help the apostles in Jerusalem, Stephen became the first martyr in the church.
Acts 6–7

Thomas

One of the twelve apostles, Thomas was the most sceptical of the apostles when the risen Christ appeared.
Matthew 10; Mark 3; John 20–21

Timothy

A young friend and convert of Paul, Timothy went on Paul's second missionary journey, and later became a leader of the church in Ephesus. Paul wrote two letters to him.
Acts 16–17; 1 and 2 Timothy

Titus

A gentile convert, sent as a missionary to Crete. Paul wrote a letter to him.
2 Corinthians 2; Galatians 2; Titus

Index

All photographs commissioned by Three's Company, except p. 9 (Jamie Simson), pp. 21, 30 (British Museum), and p. 25 (Clifford Shirley).